Guess What I'm Feeling

CBT Activity Book for Kids

Written & Illustrated by Anjula Evans, M.T.S.C.

Children's Books by Anjula Evans

I Kicked the Ball in Gym Class: Self Esteem & Being Different

School Day Worries: The Link Between Thoughts & Anxiety

The Anti-Bullying Project

Why Is Skin Color Different?

Where is My Gigi? Losing Someone You Love

What Is Foster Care? Emma's Journey

Guess How I'm Feeling

The Super-Hero Survival Guide

Novels by Anjula Evans

Antares Trap

COVID ICU

Marked Exchange

Paperback Edition ISBN 978-1-989803-25-7
Hardcover Edition ISBN 978-1-989803-26-4

Dedicated to those who keep persevering,
even when things are tough.

HAPPY

LAUGHS

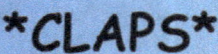
CLAPS

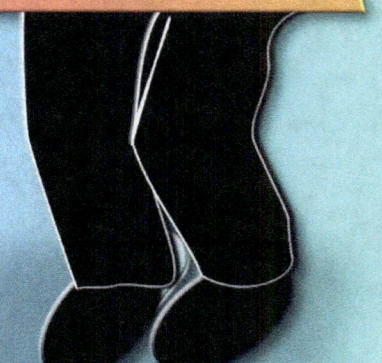

DANCES

Feeling: _____

Where do I feel it?

Helping Situations

Sometimes when these things happen...
(Draw or write)

...I Feel Happy!

SAD

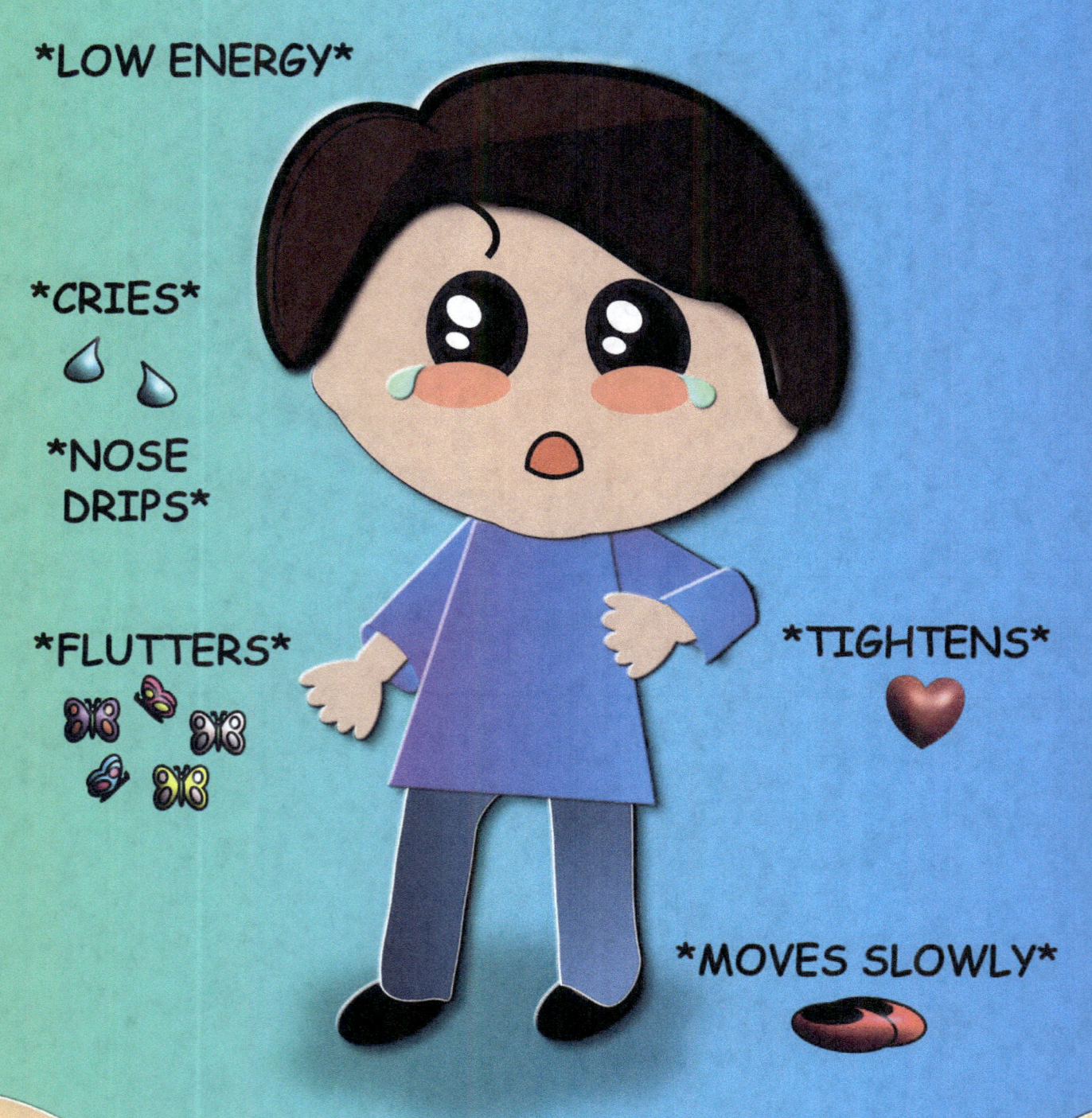

Feeling: _____

Where do I feel it?

Linking Thinking

Activity: Change a negative thought to a positive one

When I think:

Do you notice that every thought has a matching feeling?

I'll change my thought to:

Discovery: My thoughts are linked to feelings.

Conclusion: If I change my thoughts, my feelings will change too!

Linking Thinking

Activity: Change a negative thought to a positive one

When I think:

Feeling: _____

I'll change my thought to:

Feeling: _____

If I change my thoughts, my feelings will change too!

Thought Hunt

Situation: asking to play

Thoughts: They won't want to play with me

Feelings: sadness, loneliness

Thought Change: Maybe they would like me to play with them

New Feelings: confident, happy

Thought Hunt

Situation:

_____

Thoughts:

Feelings:

_____

Thought Change:

New Feelings:

Sometimes when this happens...

(Draw or write)

...I Feel Sad

Something that Could Help:

(Draw or write)

Guess what I'm feeling

ANXIETY

TIGHTNESS AROUND HEAD

HEAD FEELS LIGHT

LOOKS BLURRY

SWEATS

FAST BREATHING

TIGHTENS

FLUTTERS

NUMBNESS

RUSHES

Feeling: _____

Where do I feel it?

Linking Thinking

Activity: Change a negative thought to a positive one

When I think:

Do you notice that every thought has a matching feeling?

I'll change my thought to:

ConfiDence

I can do it!

Discovery: My thoughts are linked to feelings.

Conclusion: If I change my thoughts, my feelings will change too!

Linking Thinking

Activity: Change a negative thought to a positive one

When I think:

Feeling: _____

I'll change my thought to:

Feeling: _____

If I change my thoughts, my feelings will change too!

Thought Hunt

Situation: about to do a test

Thoughts: I practiced, but what if I don't do well?

Feelings: anxiety, nervousness, worry

Thought Change: I practiced, so I <u>will</u> do well

New Feelings: confident, ready, happy

Thought Hunt

Situation:

_____

Thoughts:

Feelings:

_____

Thought Change:

New Feelings:

Helping Situations

Sometimes when this happens...

(Draw or write)

...I Feel Anxious

Something that Could Help:

(Draw or write)

ANGER

FROWNS

HANDS ON HIPS

STOMPS

Feeling: _____

Where do I feel it?

Linking Thinking

Activity: Change a negative thought to a positive one

When I think:

Do you notice that every thought has a matching feeling?

I'll change my thought to:

Independence

I sometimes get to do what I want to

Discovery: My thoughts are linked to feelings.

Conclusion: If I change my thoughts, my feelings will change too!

Linking Thinking

Activity: Change a negative thought to a positive one

When I think:

Feeling: _____

I'll change my thought to:

Feeling: _____

If I change my thoughts, my feelings will change too!

Thought Hunt

Situation: not doing favorite activity

Thoughts: I never get to do what I want to

Feelings: anger, no choices

Thought Change: I sometimes get to do what I want to

New Feelings: independent, happy

Thought Hunt

Situation:

_____

Thoughts:

Feelings:

_____

Thought Change:

New Feelings:

Sometimes when this happens...
(Draw or write)

...I Feel Angry

Something that Could Help:
(Draw or write)

FRIGHTENED

SCREAMS

FLUTTERS

FAST-BEATING

RUNS OR FREEZES

Feeling: _____

Where do I feel it?

Linking Thinking

Activity: Change a negative thought to a positive one

When I think:

SCARED

I'm afraid something terrible will happen!

Do you notice that every thought has a matching feeling?

I'll change my thought to:

Discovery: My thoughts are linked to feelings.

Conclusion: If I change my thoughts, my feelings will change too!

Linking Thinking

Activity: Change a negative thought to a positive one

When I think:

Feeling: _____

I'll change my thought to:

Feeling: _____

If I change my thoughts, my feelings will change too!

Thought Hunt

Situation: about to go to school

Thoughts: What if something terrible happens?

Feelings: fear

Thought Change: Usually something good happens

New Feelings: reassurance

Thought Hunt

Situation:

_____

Thoughts:

Feelings:

_____

Thought Change:

New Feelings:

Sometimes when this happens...

(Draw or write)

...I Feel Frightened

Something that Could Help:

(Draw or write)

SHY

BLUSHES

FLUTTERS

TIGHTENS

Feeling: _____

Where do I feel it?

Linking Thinking

Activity: Change a negative thought to a positive one

When I think:

Selfconsciousness

They might not like me

Do you notice that every thought has a matching feeling?

I'll change my thought to:

Engaging

I'm going to be very friendly

Discovery: My thoughts are linked to feelings.

Conclusion: If I change my thoughts, my feelings will change too!

Linking Thinking

Activity: Change a negative thought to a positive one

When I think:

Feeling: _____

I'll change my thought to:

Feeling: _____

If I change my thoughts, my feelings will change too!

Thought Hunt

Situation: meeting someone new

Thoughts: What if he doesn't like me?

Feelings: selfconsciousness

Thought Change: I am very friendly and likeable.

New Feelings: selfconfidence

Thought Hunt

Situation:

_____

Thoughts:

Feelings:

_____

Thought Change:

New Feelings:

Sometimes when this happens...

(Draw or write)

...I Feel Shy

Something that Could Help:

(Draw or write)

SICK, TIRED, BORED

NO ENERGY

POSTURE SLUMPS

SLOW MOVING

Feeling: _____

Where do I feel it?

Linking Thinking

Activity: Change a negative thought to a positive one

When I think:

BOREDOM

There's nothing to do

Do you notice that every thought has a matching feeling?

I'll change my thought to:

Creativity

There's always something interesting to do!

Discovery: My thoughts are linked to feelings.

Conclusion: If I change my thoughts, my feelings will change too!

Linking Thinking

Activity: Change a negative thought to a positive one

When I think:

Feeling: _____

I'll change my thought to:

Feeling: _____

If I change my thoughts, my feelings will change too!

Thought Hunt

Situation: it's a rainy day outside

Thoughts: There's nothing to do today

Feelings: boredom, restlessness

Thought Change: There are things to do. I just have to find them.

New Feelings: productivity, creativity

Thought Hunt

Situation:

_____

Thoughts:

Feelings:

_____

Thought Change:

New Feelings:

Sometimes when this happens...

(Draw or write)

...I Feel Sick, Tired, or Bored

Something that Could Help:

(Draw or write)

EXCITED

FULL OF ENERGY

CHEERS

CLAPS

FLUTTERS

JUMPS
DANCES

Feeling: _____

Where do I feel it?

Sometimes when these things happen...

(Draw or write)

...I Feel Excited!

Helping Situations

Sometimes when this happens...
(Draw or write)

...I Feel _____

Something that Could Help:
(Draw or write)

WHERE DO I FEEL IT?

HAPPY

LAUGHS

CLAPS

DANCES

SAD

CRIES

NOSE DRIPS

TIGHTENS

FLUTTERS

LOW ENERGY

ANGRY

FROWNS

STOMPS

HANDS ON HIPS

FRIGHTENED

SCREAMS

FAST-BEATING

FLUTTERS

RUNS OR FREEZES

WHERE DO I FEEL IT?

EXCITED

FULL OF ENERGY

CLAPS

JUMPS

DANCES

SHY

BLUSHES

TIGHTENS

FLUTTERS

ANXIOUS

*TIGHTENS

TIGHTENS

FLUTTERS

RUSHES

SICK AND TIRED

NO ENERGY

POSTURE SLUMPS

SLOW-MOVING

I NEED:

TO DRAW

TO EXERCISE

A CUDDLE

MUSIC

I NEED:

TO TALK

A NAP

A FRIEND

JUST MYSELF

When I feel: I can try:

How many ideas can you try?

When I feel:

I can try: